Home Again

Betty Fountain Yamakuchi

ISBN:
0615481884

ISBN-13:
978-0615481883

(Sloopy Publishing)

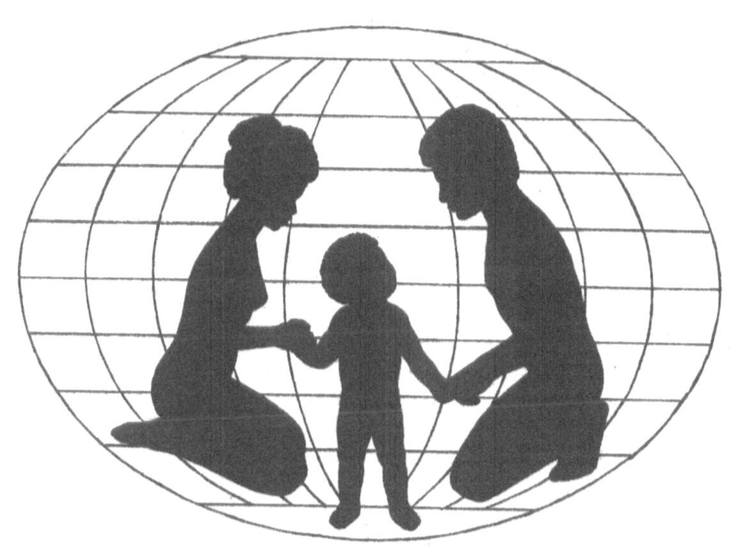

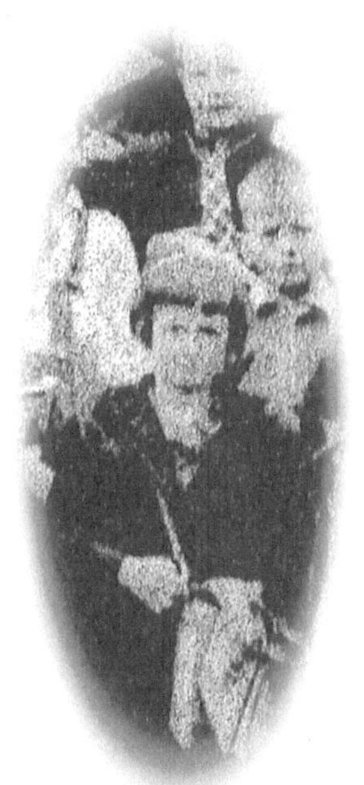

↑ me 1ST Grade 1936

Home Again *

I have come home again
Where the tall trees and
Crape Myrtles grow
Where white magnolia blossoms
Grace the land
Where two rivers meet
To form one– and
Weeping Willows touch
The water's Edge
To see the ever changing
Beauty of each days sunset
And feel the warmth of summer
Linger into Fall
Here people smile
And children are friendly
And unafraid to speak
My heart never left
Though my body roamed
I've been many places
But here in the foothills
Are the paths of Childhood
Here is home.

[illegible signature]
– 2002

Scenes of Youth

As time grows shorter
I recreate ______ scenes
From my distant youth.
The magic of the playground
In the morning sun
As young girls gather
Around the swings
To watch the boys arrive.
Then the ball field
Would come alive
With hustling players
Catching flies
Warming up
And swinging bats
Hearing the chatter
Old men stop
To sit on benches
Just to watch_____ 'cause
Baseball lasts forever.

Come to the cave
It's up on the hill
Crawl in and explore
Where the Cherokee did.
There's an apple orchard
round the bend-
The apples are green,
But the tomatoes are ripe
Run! The old woman
Will chase you out of sight.
We ate ten tomatoes one day
Yes, it's true!
Forbidden fruit tastes better.

Down a wooded path
Hand in hand
Three or four couples
Every weekend
Sometimes we kissed
But never more
Than an intimate whisper
Or maybe a hug-
I remember that,
Way back then-
We were the innocents.

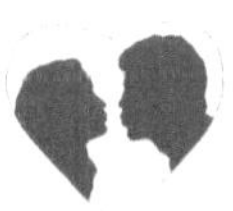

The mill whistle blew
(It's silent now)
I still see him walking
In his seersucker suit
Coming to see my sister
In the late afternoon.
If they sat on the couch
I would intervene-
Chattering and combing
His black wavy hair.

Here in my memory
Still full of life
The sweetest friends still play.
Their youthful faces appear to me
Not timeworn, old, and gray.
I can visit with them.
Relive with them
And the years roll away
My mind and body is young again
In reveries of yesterday.

Dream of Life

To be in that ecstatic state
    of surrender
Aware of a special glance
    thrilled by a voice~~
Coming near to embrace,
    to adore.
Turning a lovers faults and
    flaws into virtues
Magnificent feeling of
    motion that is still
As love the aristocracy of
    all human feelings
Casts out the demon hate
    and its violent mental armies.

Then we know why song and
    dance were born
Smiles flashed and colorful
    clothes adorned.
Spirit unchained rushes out
    to answer yes
And rivers of the soul flow
    young and clean
Carrying the immortal blessed
    state of loving.
The lasting dream of life.

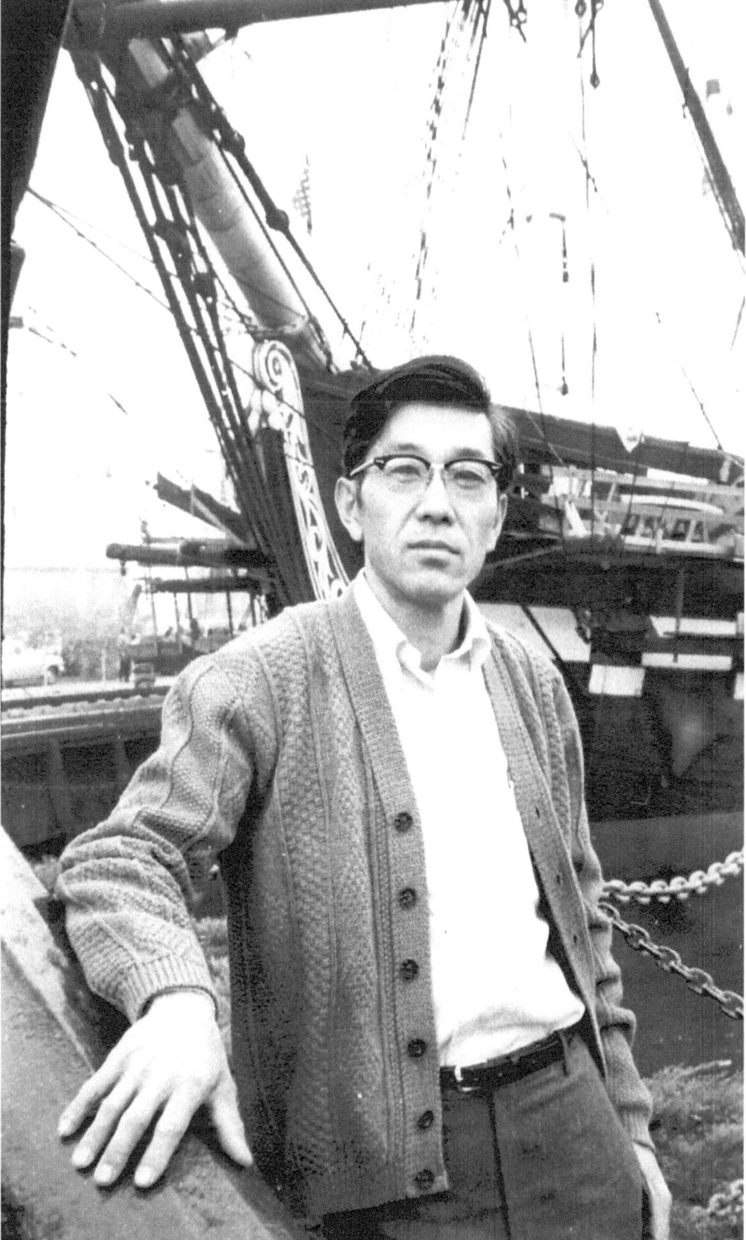

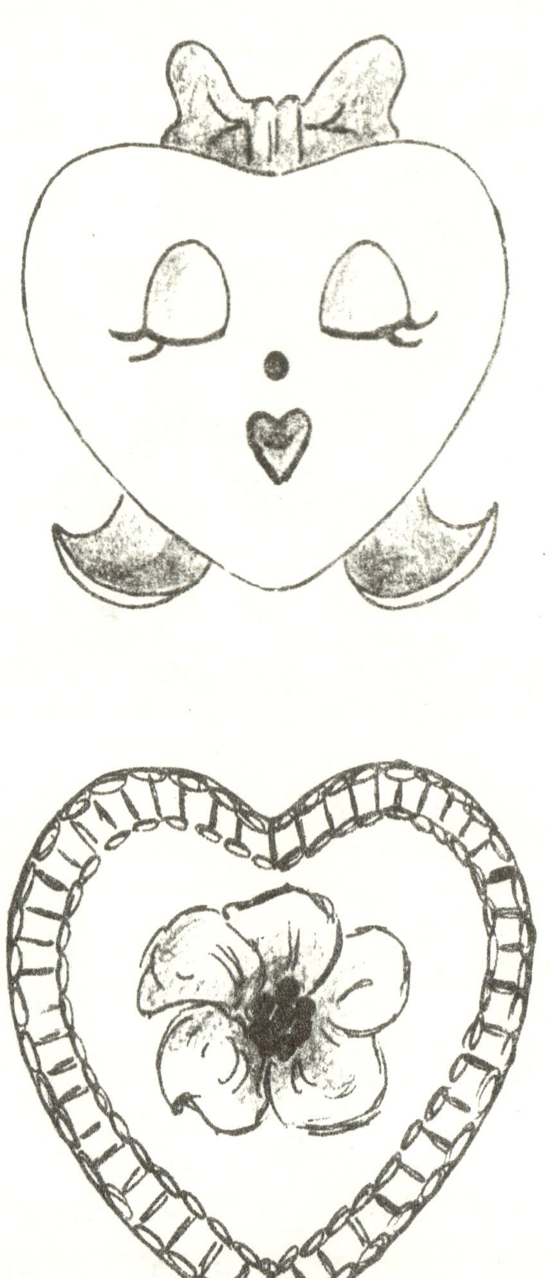

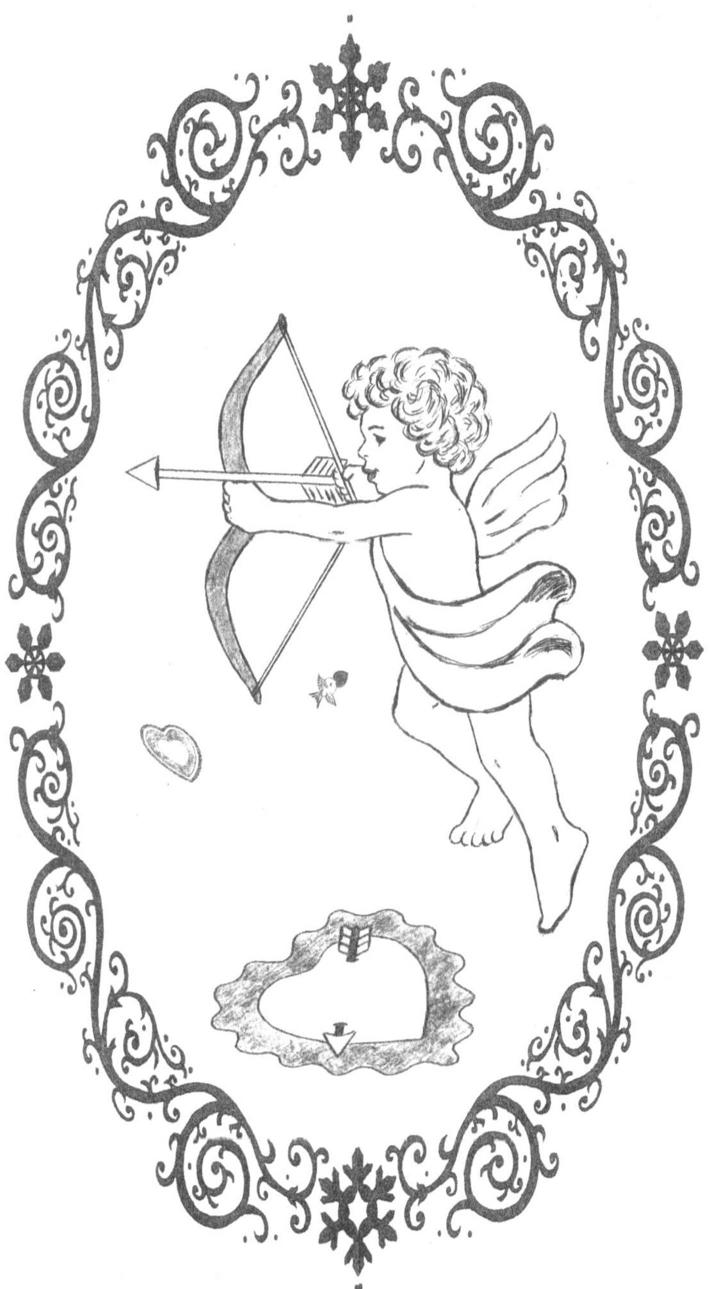

Chicago

From all the world to this city come people,
And they become it's people.
Alert industrious, spirited-
Bringing talents, ideas, bearing dreams.
Here, unbound by social order, lives hope
A dimension of venture
Room left to try out and to realize
With elements somehow mixed
To keep it infinite.

Come to all parts - know it's people
Alert to the news, learning from the past.
The free thinkers in the coffee houses-
Listen to them talk.
The young politician uprooting the encumbent-
Hear him!
The intellectual's innovations
Shaping change by confrontation-
Designer, artist, architect...creating
The dark citizen becoming articulate
Turning his own history; appearing everywhere.

Go walk Oak Street Beach-
Stand at State and Madison.
Catch an 'L' or Subway.
Feel pushed, unimportant, alone

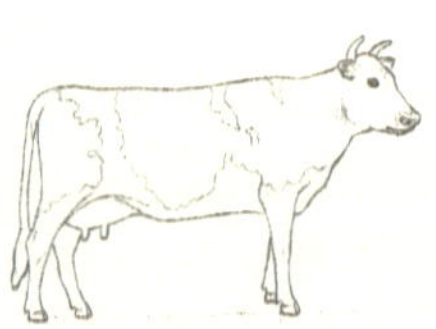

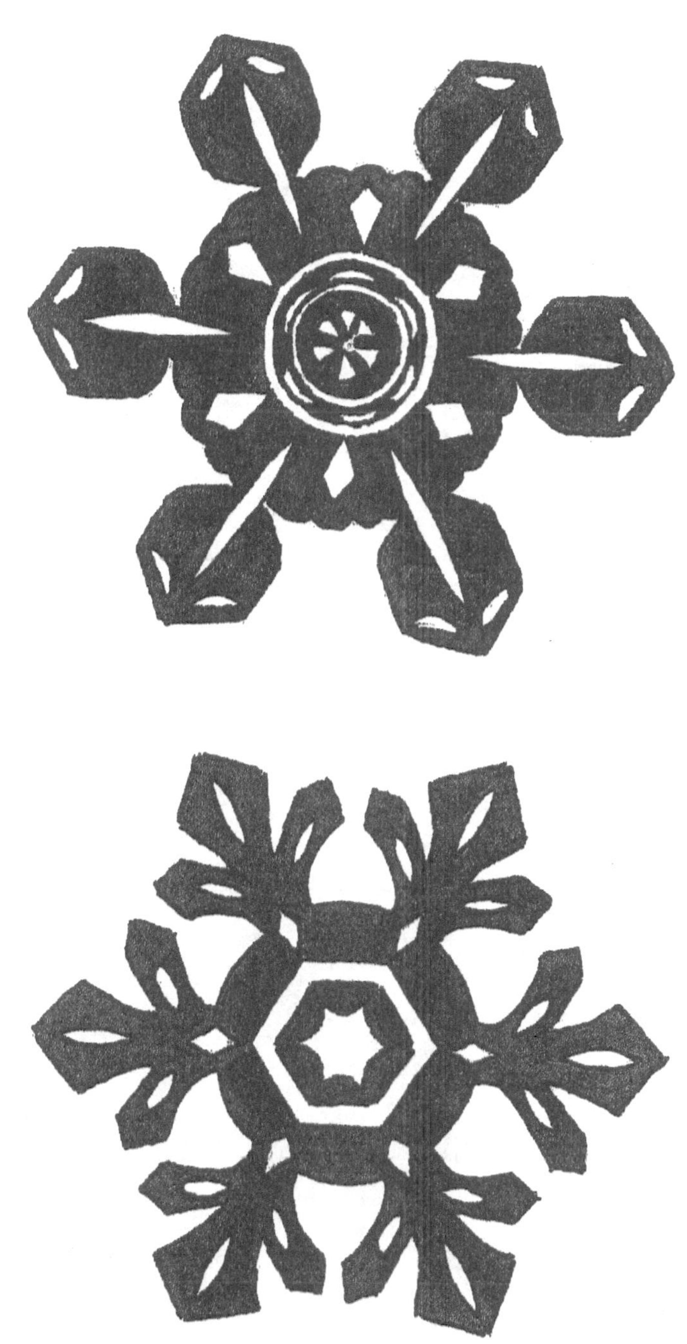

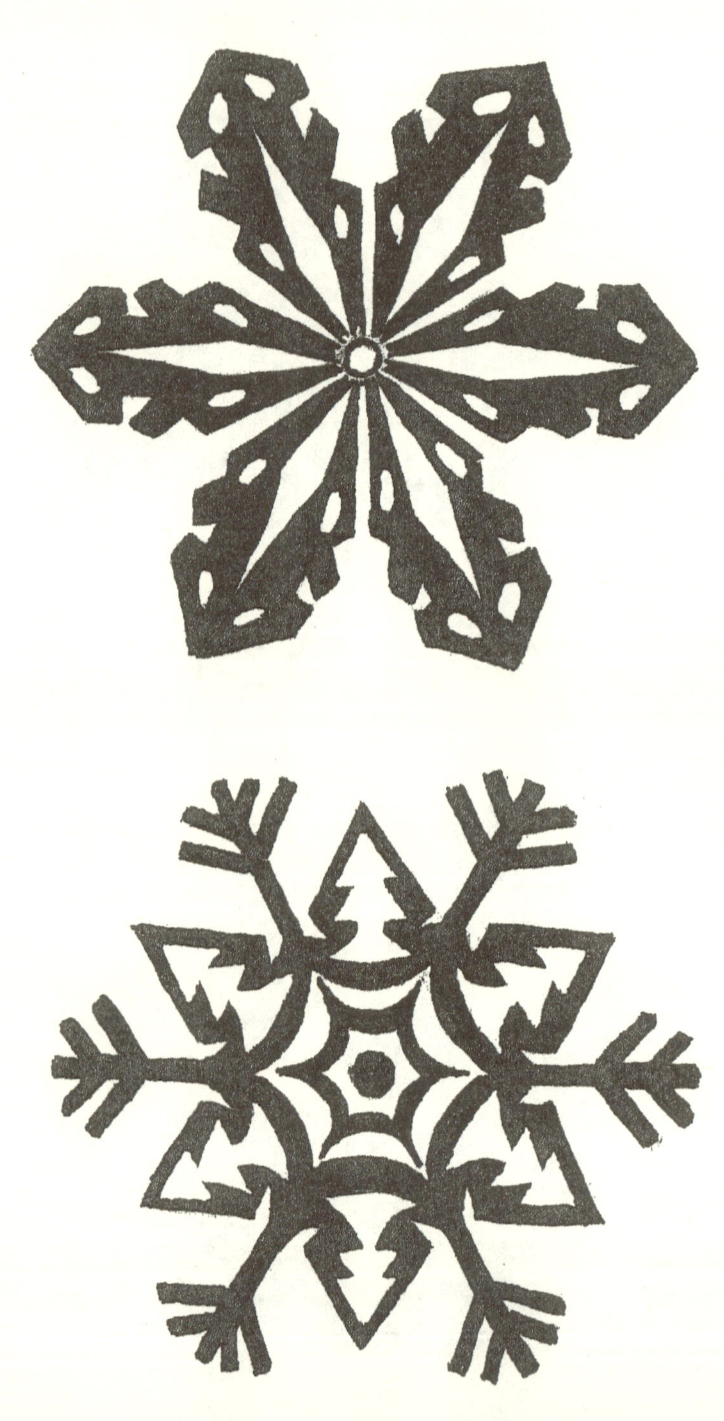

For there's a growling animal march by day,
And the nightlife of lights flash on spenders-
Middle-aged couples with pretense of youth;
Youth with pretense of suavity.
Know the city at daybreak, sweetly quiet;
Embrace the city while it's sleeping,
For it's gone again, too soon, on the next day's race.

Rectitude was never a claim here
The lazy, the lawbreaker, the vulgar-
They live here too.
Woven into the scene with faulty threads.
Never-the-less as intrinsic as the builders.
But don't be afraid to take the city on-
For it's a tough city
Founded by rugged men.
Willed to rugged sons.

Chicago - human, vital, perpetual-
Where jets zoom.
Skybound buildings appear overnight.
Crimes - crowds - deadlines.
Where workers work, artists see life,
Arrivers experience hope.
A busy city on a lake front.
Living intimately with nature-
With elements somehow mixed
To keep it infinite.

Betty J Yamaguchi
circa 60's

Friendship

Bring me your pain
And hidden tears-
This will be our bond.
Lost and confused?
Come here -near-
Let me hear your voice.
Don't turn away - but to me.
My love is broad and supple.

You are to me joy,
But more - still more.
Take all you can from me,
For that's what I am doing.
Let's share while we're together,
And when you leave-leave-
But know me.
My door is always open.

To say that friendship is less
Than other loves would be wrong.
In it's purest form it is superior,
Existing for no other reason but choice.
Love is given without having
To meet rules of conduct.
Wishing only the best
For its recipient.

It may be a fun filled
Strong camaraderie-
It can be achingly
Tender and warm.
Whatever the need friends
Have for each other
A delicate gift goes back and forth,
Untarnished, cared for, surprisingly new.

You may have several friends
In a lifetime -
They bare the same soul -
That carries human understanding.
We an give our friend a look inside -
Dreams, fears, weaknesses -
The way others would not
Want to see us.
All knowing it mysteriously survives -
Still reaches out -
We are not alone.
We are loved and not alone.

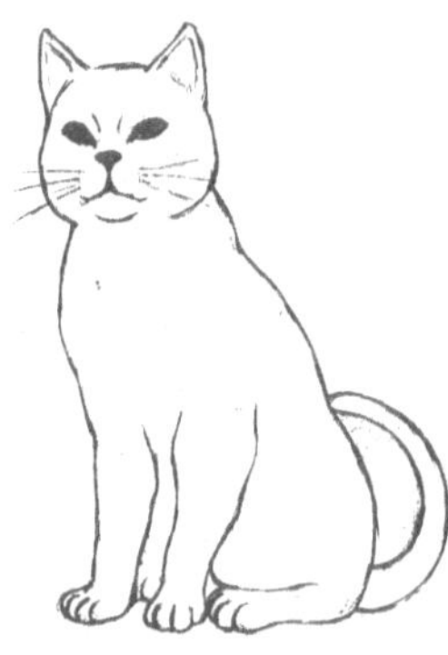

Felicia

This modern world is wrong for you.
You are set out of time.
The ugly and brutal brush too close.
You should be sung.
You belong in a summer place
where flowers grow ~
By a soft brook
where romance visits.
Gentle strength should know
your touch.
You belong to a dance
where bodies stay young.

But nature has a region
where laughter mingles with tears
and a thousand things change places.
Life comes down hard
after the morning light ~
strikes its blows
to the partner of Pan ~
toughening up the mind
unsettles its lyrics ~
changing forever the games of Spring.

Ruth

Beginning in biblical times, and through
the annals of history
moved the true woman.
For nature chose her, gave her orders,
then celebrated in her virtues.
She was placed in the middle with a
cycloramic view.
She saw the splendors and terrors.
Given no special talent to warp her-
She was instead put on intimate terms
with life - to know sorrow, comfort
friends, hold children, love men.
In fields mountains, deserts, and streets
She lived everywhere
And her truth was audible
to those who listened _
For she touched people with an artistry
known only by the warmest of women.
Still she was wise enough to retain mystery
and a playful child nestled inside that
wise and seasoned head.
Committed - indestructible - She worked and
survived each generation.
No history was made without her.

From a distance and with perspective,
I see all women in one woman.
In a white smile, dark curls, and a
voice that awakens all senses -
I turn with others to touch
what we love.
and we call her Ruth.

I

In my mind I hold a great weight,
It is my own description.
Destined to struggle with the conflict
Of what I am and what I want to be-
Murmurs of other voices join my shadow,
I want, I need, I wish-
I is the saddest word in language.

I have never been able to look at a face
And not feel another's pain.
I know I am everyone.
I am the ugly who wants admiration,
But can't attract.
I am the cripple who wants to dance.
The no-fault sick who dreams of health.
I am shy, unprepared,
Lamely I try with unskilled tools.
I am old, obese, lonely,
Wishing to be something else.
An accident of birth
I find no direction-
I am alienated, angry, hated, a loser,
Unable to be understood.
I lie, I cheat, I misuse, I dissipate,
Struggling for what I don't understand
I am trapped in a circle of wrong moves.
I weave to survive and
Wish for outside change.

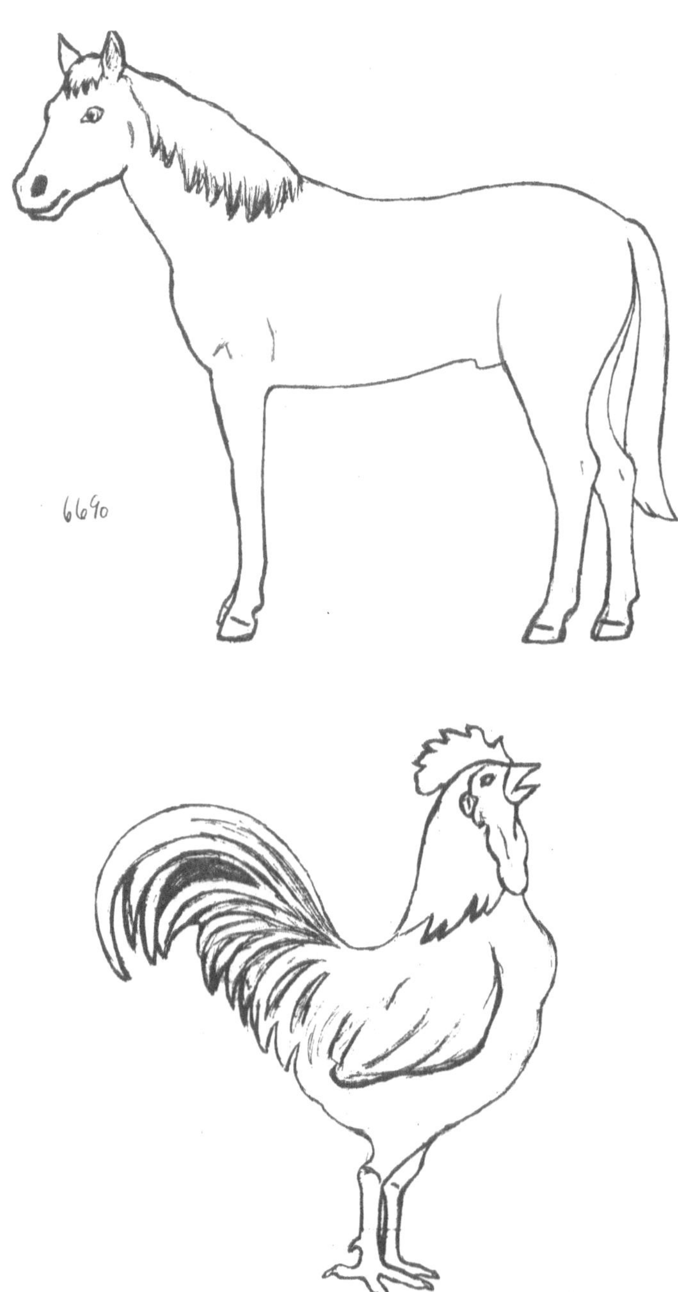
6690

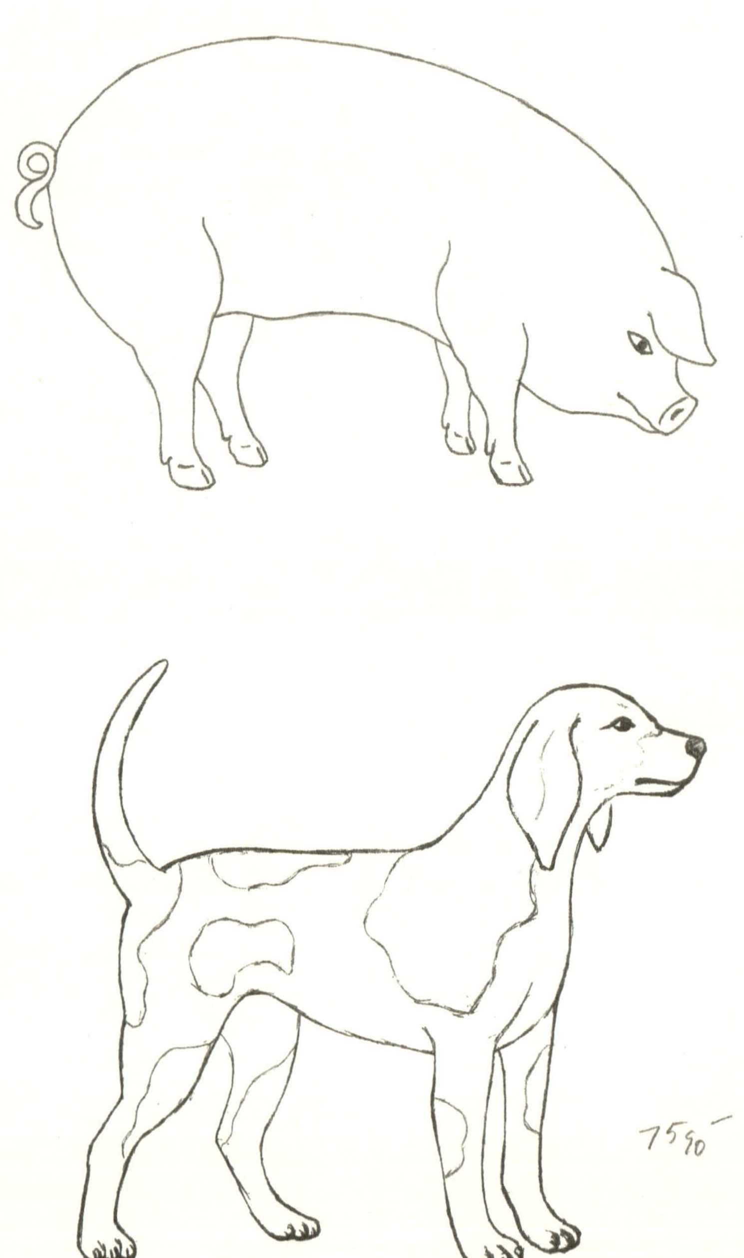

I

No one loves me-
In memory no one ever did.
What a toll on the spirit
To seek and never attain.
What does this do to judgement?

In awe of the minute and the vastness-
Humbled I kneel
With all religions-
Weep for those who commit
Crimes against themselves
And doubt there is a God.

On stage I see the brave, lucky,
Beautiful, successful, intelligent, the serene.
I worship at their image-
In fantasy I am there too.
Life is a cruel director
Casting the roles without merit.
Everyone must audition and
All give audience to the play.

The Terrorist – Sept 11-2001

Sons of darkness
Moved among us
Shared our freedom
And lived in peace
Life was good
But their role was different
They had Trained for death
And it's Holy reward
But the gates of heaven
Were closed against them
No one could enter
With blood on their hands.

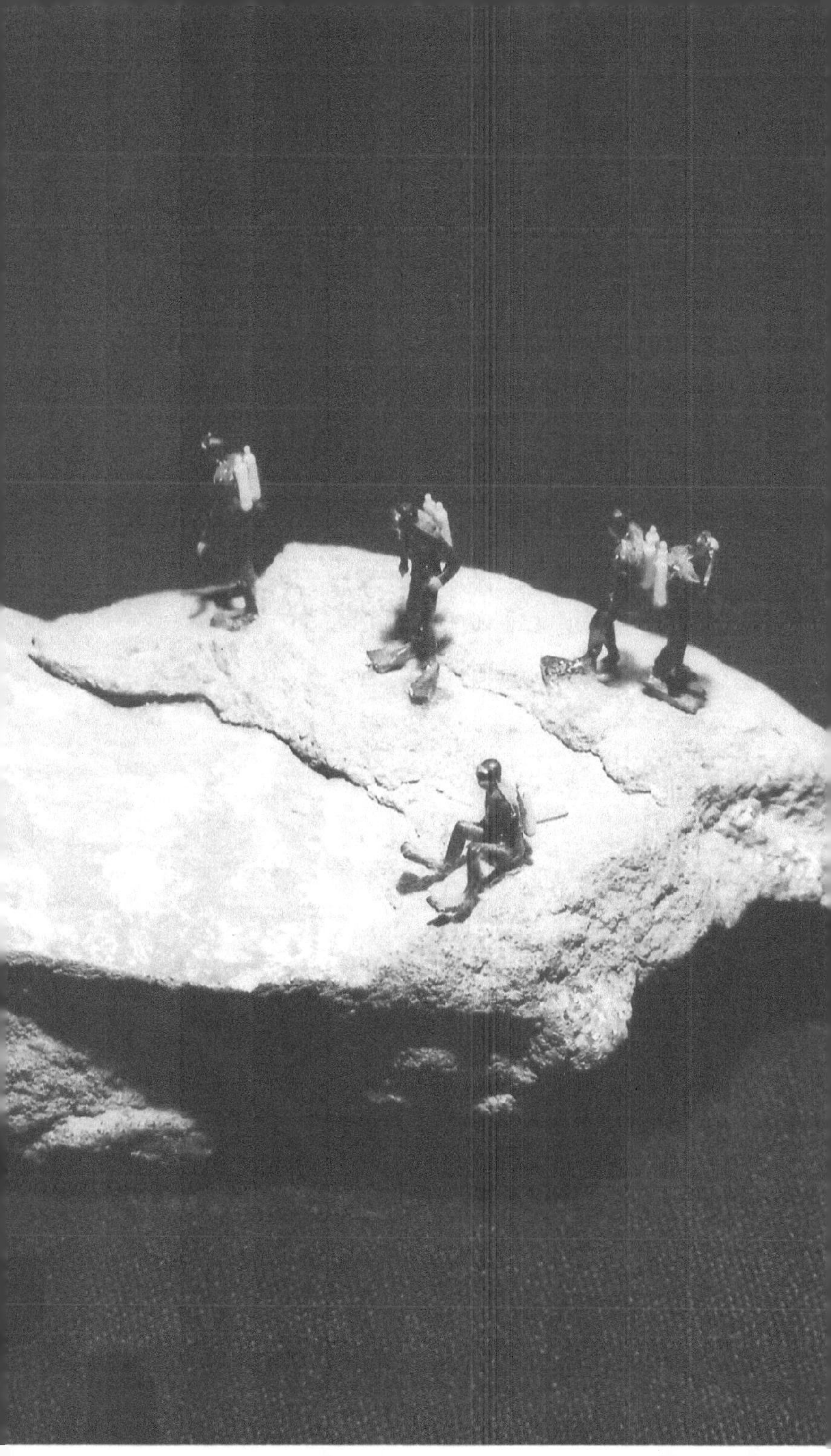

TO SEE

TO SEE
Never have my eyes been
As capable as they are now
Right and wrong stand apart
So clearly
Even in their complex and deceptive forms
The growing of children
Take shape
And explain things

There is a central theme
Being played
Made up of countless counterpoints
That I understand
I follow orgins at a glance
Tracing reason by reason
Finding why.

People - muscled and moving
Wrapped up in minuteness
Their circle not touching many
But the circles they touch
Touch other circles
Making Their sounds
In and out of harmony
With all circles

Little forces move
Changing some completely
Some partly - Touching others never
Big forces make by sweep
Change so complete
Little that was - is left in place

I see beside me, around, in back
ALL Shapes, heights, walks, sounds
Know everyone by these
I could close my eyes
I would still Know
All my senses are as wise
As my eyes are now.

Suffering – I see so much
Falling on the wrong people
Making virtues hard to follow
And opportunity jerked at
By other means

Those who cry
Cry for the lost way
Those who laugh
Do so to stop crying
Only the innocent
And truly holy dance

In the end
Because I see
Never have I been more unhappy
Still I can't run away
I work Harder
For never have I been stronger
And inside
I turn to Art to worship.

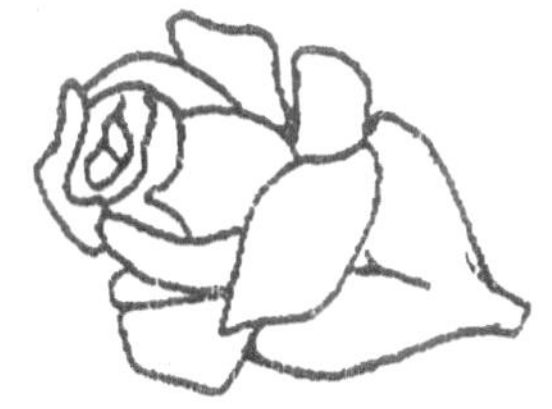

When We Were Young

We saw the world
In a robins nest
A smile could
Hold such passion
A lock of hair
In a scrapbook
And under it a gem of wisdom
Lyrics of songs
You could sing
And years later still remember
No one wanted
To quit school
And everyone went to the movies

I don't think we
Were always happy
But each of us
Carried a dream
We stayed young
A little longer
And grew stronger
For what was to be

Dedicated to the class of '48

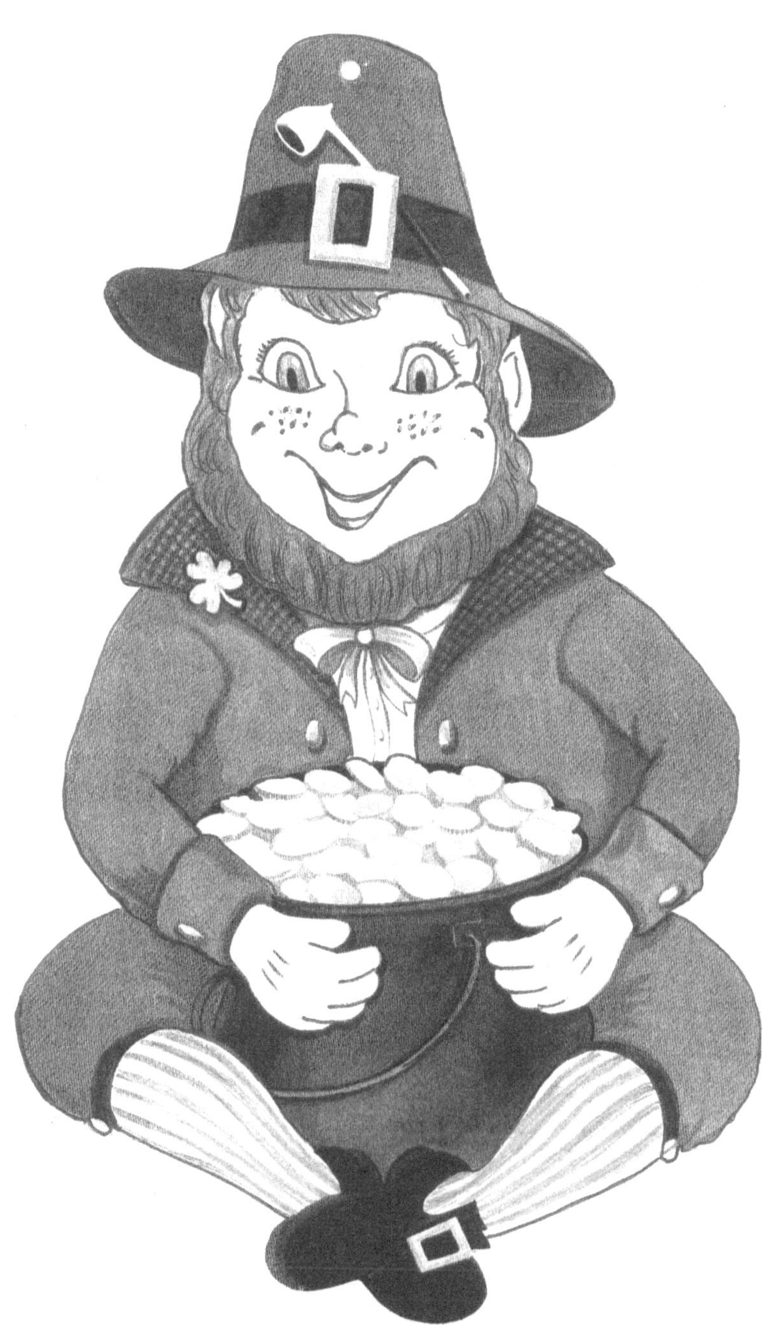

www.ingramcontent.com/pod-product-compliance
Lightning Source LLC
LaVergne TN
LVHW050951080826
845145LV00004B/1465
* 9 7 8 0 6 1 5 4 8 1 8 8 3 *